The Triangle Shirtwaist Factory Fire: The History and Legacy of New York City's Deadliest Industrial Disaster

By Charles River Editors

About Charles River Editors

Charles River Editors provides superior editing and original writing services across the digital publishing industry, with the expertise to create digital content for publishers across a vast range of subject matter. In addition to providing original digital content for third party publishers, we also republish civilization's greatest literary works, bringing them to new generations of readers via ebooks.

Sign up here to receive updates about free books as we publish them, and visit Our Kindle Author Page to browse today's free promotions and our most recently published Kindle titles.

Introduction

A newspaper illustration marking the windows where women jumped to escape the fire

The Triangle Shirtwaist Factory Fire (March 25, 1911)

"Word had spread through the East Side, by some magic of terror, that the plant of the Triangle Waist Company was on fire and that several hundred workers were trapped. Horrified and helpless, the crowds — I among them — looked up at the burning building, saw girl after girl appear at the reddened windows, pause for a terrified moment, and then leap to the pavement below, to land as mangled, bloody pulp. This went on for what seemed a ghastly eternity. Occasionally a girl who had hesitated too long was licked by pursuing flames and, screaming with clothing and hair ablaze, plunged like a living torch to the street. Life nets held by the firemen were torn by the impact of the falling bodies. The emotions of the crowd were indescribable. Women were hysterical, scores fainted; men wept as, in paroxysms of frenzy, they hurled themselves against the police lines." – Louis Waldman, a New York State Assemblyman

During the afternoon of March 25, 1911, shortly before workers at the Triangle Shirtwaist Factory in the Asch Building left for the day, a fire broke out in a scrap bin on the 8th floor of the building. Fires were nothing new in such situations, and the industrial journal *The Insurance Monitor* noted that garment factories were "fairly saturated with moral hazard," but on this particular day, the spread of the fire to the main staircase made it impossible for workers still stuck on the 9th and 10th floors to escape. Furthermore, without today's labor regulations in place, an advanced warning of the fire never even made it to the 9th floor, despite the fire starting just one floor below, and door to the only other stairway had been locked to ensure the women working there didn't try to sneak out with stolen goods.

Some workers made it to safety on the roof and others used two elevators while they were still operating, but the fire trapped dozens, turning the entire event into a gruesome spectacle that other New Yorkers watched from the street. When the emergency fire escape collapsed as a result of the weight of the nearly 20 people on it, it sent them crashing down to the street nearly 100 feet below. But that was only the beginning of the harrowing tragedy, as the workers still trapped near windows had to make individual decisions whether to jump or let the fire creep painfully closer to them with each passing second.

Firefighters in carts drawn by horses eventually arrived, but their ladders could only reach up to the 6th floor, making it all but impossible to stop the blaze. Making matters worse, their attempts to catch jumpers with safety nets completely failed as the speed and weight of the people broke the netting. William Gunn Shepard, a reporter who witnessed the scene, later said, "I learned a new sound that day a sound more horrible than description can picture -- the thud of a speeding living body on a stone sidewalk." By the time the disaster was over, 146 workers had died, either from jumping to their deaths or from being overcome by the fire inside.

In the wake of the fire, the owners of the building were arrested and charged, and while they were acquitted of criminal charges, they were found liable in civil suits. In addition to that, there were increased calls for unionization, and New York City made a number of regulatory changes in response to not only prevent similar tragedies but dramatically increase the quality of conditions for employees in the workplace.

The Triangle Shirtwaist Factory Fire chronicles the deadly fire and the changes made in New York City after the disaster. Along with pictures of important people, places, and events, you will learn about the Triangle Shirtwaist Factory fire like never before, in no time at all.

The Triangle Shirtwaist Factory Fire: The History and Legacy of New York City's Deadliest Industrial Disaster

About Charles River Editors

Introduction

   Chapter 1: "We Came to the Triangle Shop"

   Chapter 2: "My Work Was Very Good"

   Chapter 3: "It Was a Day Bursting with Life"

   Chapter 4: "The Front Elevator Door"

   Chapter 5: "Word Had Spread…by Some Magic Terror"

   Chapter 6: "The Screams and Sobs All Around Were Deafening"

   Chapter 7: "The Rules of the Institutions Were Suspended"

   Chapter 8: "We Mourned Our Dead Comrades"

   Chapter 9: Investigations and Reforms

   Bibliography

Chapter 1: "We Came to the Triangle Shop"

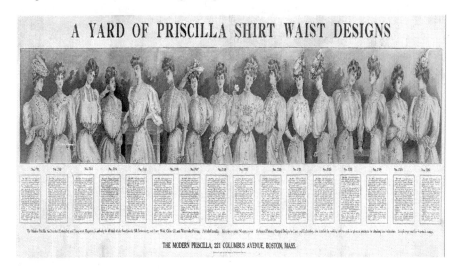

A 1906 advertisement for shirtwaists

"I worked at the Triangle Shop for nine weeks before the fire. ... I worked in the Bijou Waist Co. until the strike which lasted 5 months. Then I went to work in another place on Grand St. One day my friend said let's take a newspaper and look for a job. We came to the Triangle shop. We were taken up to the 10th floor and I asked where was the chairlady - I didn't know they had a strike. Bernstein, the manager called everybody into one big room. We packed the room and he spoke to one after another and he kept saying 'down, down, down' because they were not good enough workers for him. When he came to me and my girl-friend, he asked us if we could make a whole waist. I could not make a whole waist but with straight faces we said yes we could. ... He asked us how much we wanted. In the Bijou we made $7.50 a week so here we asked for $9. Later we were both sorry because we should have asked for $10." - Dora Appel Skalka, blouse maker on the 8th floor

Throughout much of its history, America has been known around the world as a land of opportunity, but it is an unpleasant and often overlooked fact that many of the opportunities the country offered came with a high price tag. This was certainly true for the immigrants that poured into the country during the latter half of the 19th century, for while their predecessors had been able to move west to agricultural areas where they could apply the skills they had used in their homelands, the Industrial Revolution had set off a chain of events that made many of the best opportunities in the country available only in big cities. As a result, people stopped passing through places like New York City and instead settled there, often in cramped living quarters that they could only hope to escape by working long hours working in tightly packed factories. This was especially true of girls and young women; boys and young men might find heavy labor along the docks or on ships, but girls were considered too weak for such work and instead spent up to 12 hours a day operating sewing machines, weaving looms and other dangerous equipment.

Thus, each Monday through Saturday, the streets of New York City were flooded with young women in crisply starched blouses and cheap serge skirts, as well as little girls still in braids and pinafores, heading to work in the city's factories. Tens of thousands poured in from the tenements of the Lower East Side of Manhattan, leaving behind mothers and aunts and younger siblings who depended on their earnings for survival. Most of them spoke heavily accented English, but when speaking amongst themselves, listeners would hear various languages and dialects, ranging from Russian to Italian to Yiddish.

The lucky ones had someone older to walk with them and see them safely to their work, at least on their first day. One woman later remembered, "Father had to take me to the shop and not be late for his own work. I was eager to begin life on my own responsibility but was also afraid. 'Don't look so frightened,' he said." Mary Domsky-Abrams, who worked at the Triangle Shirtwaist Factory, recalled, "There were very few men in the shop; the hundreds of girls were mostly Jewish, a few were Italians. I and many others were still practically 'greenhorns,' we had been in the country only a year or less. For many, as for me, it was only the second job, for others the first that they had had. Most of us were not yet 20 years old."

As bad as a fire was, the general working conditions at the Triangle Shirtwaist Company were not as bad as those in many other factories during the early 20th century. One of the young women who worked there, Mary Domsky-Abrams, explained, "Working conditions at the Triangle shop were quite bearable, for those days. Wage rates weren't too bad; we had won them by fighting for them, through stoppages, etc. The shop, both on the eighth and ninth floors, was light and airy, and was, more or less, clean, although pieces of cloth from the cutting room were strewn on the floor. The bosses held themselves aloof from the workers; we never saw them in the shop. They had their offices on the tenth floor, and rarely showed themselves. We dealt only with the manager."

The women who worked in the factory got to work each morning by 8:00 sharp, making their way to the top three floors of the 10 story Asch building. Sylvia Kimeldorf, a tucker who worked on the 8th floor, noted, "Before I worked for the Triangle Co. I worked for Winter Co. on Wooster Street. I got paid by Triangle, $10 a week, flat rate, for six days a week, including Saturdays. They had a real speed-up system so that when they gave you the goods, let's say 60 yard, they fixed the time it should lake to do the work. When we left the shop we were searched. We had to open our bags to show what was in them. They even had a matron in the ladies room who would check to see how long you stayed in the ladies' room and if you had any material on you."

An early 20th century photo of the building

A picture of the building today

The days were long, and the work was backbreaking. Celia Saltz later remembered her early days at the factory, saying, "We worked on bundles of 2, 2 1/2, or 3 dozen blouses. They were very good shirts. When I began to work for myself I joined the backs to the fronts. We also made the tucks on the fronts. The cutters took up less than half of the floor but we never went near them because somebody would think that we were looking to take something."

After working a long day, the women left at 5:00 and made their way downstairs by one elevator, but they had to suffer a final humiliation each day before they finally got out the door.

Mary Domsky-Abrams explained, "In the morning, when we were going up to work, both elevators (front and back) would be operating. But on leaving, only the one in the back was allowed to run. This was because the company directed a watchman to search the girls' pocketbooks, in which we used to carry our lunches. As the bosses wanted to save the expense of having another watchman at the front, they allowed only one exit to be used for all three floors. We considered it to be the greatest insult to have to open our pocketbooks and show that we weren't stealing anything. The bosses' lawyers said this was necessary because the workers brought along these pocketbooks with the intention of slipping out some "waists."

Many of those working at the factory were even younger than the age of 10, the youngest age allowed by law. Ida Kornweiser, an operator and sleeve setter from the 9th floor, recalled, "I worked on the 9th floor for a little less than one year at the time of the fire. I was an operator and sleeve setter on section work. I worked about 4-5 weeks without pay, then I began to make about $3 or $4. a week from the inside contractor who took me up. I must have been a child at that time because I remember that when the inspector used to come they would push me into the toilet to hide."

Naturally, those in charge were careful to no draw attention to their violations of the law. Saltz explained, "A lot of us were very young like children at that time. When the inspectors would come we would hide in the baskets or big boxes. I looked young too and Bernstein would tell me to get up from my machine when the inspectors came."

Moreover, the working conditions were often made less pleasant by those in charge. Domsky-Abrams noted, "Then we saw the manager approaching, so we quickly ended our conversation. His name was Bonstein (sic); I think he was a relative of the bosses (we never saw them). He was a short person, with broad shoulders and piercing eyes. He always had a cynical smile on his face. He was strict and unscrupulous with the workers. But I must admit he was very clever, and very apt for his job. When he would see a group of us in conversation, he would sidle over, calmly, with the cynical smile on his face, on the chance that he might be able to pick up a word or two of what we were saying. Of course, as soon as we saw him approach, we would immediately change the subject and start talking about theater, concerts, opera, etc. One day he said to us: 'It is a remarkable thing! We're living in such wonderful times! When did workers ever know about theaters and concerts? And now--they occupy almost all the seats at performances...' And we replied, 'Mr. Bonstein (sic), the workers are more entitled to enjoy these than the bosses are.' As he came near us on that fateful day, one girl asked him, 'Mr. Bonstein (sic), why is there no water in the buckets? In case of a fire, there would be nothing with which to fight it,' He became enraged at our group of price committee members, and with inhuman anger replied: 'If you'll burn, there'll be something to put out the fire.'"

Pictures of the factory's owners, Isaac Harris and Max Blanck

In spite of the difficulties each experienced, the young men and women who worked at the factory often found ways to lighten their burdens. Rose Hauser, who worked on the 9th floor, discussed one such diversion: "On the floor a gong used to ring when the day was over. About five minutes before quitting time I sneaked into the dressing room. There were a few girls in the dressing room. I used to sing a lot in the shop, some of the girls asked me to sing a song while we were getting dressed. They asked me to sing -- I still remember the name of the song – 'Every Little Movement Has a Meaning of Its Own'. They insisted that I sing so I did my little act in the dressing room."

Chapter 2: "My Work Was Very Good"

"I worked at Triangle for about a year before the fire. I started first to work for a contractor in the shop and I made about $3 a week. There were lots of inside contractors in the shop - each one hired his own girls. We did not know the prices for the work, only he did and only he paid us. I worked up from $3 until I was making as much as $10 a week. About a week after I was working for 6 months, I went to Bernstein who was the manager and I told him I had enough of working for a subcontractor. I told him I wanted to work for myself so he gave me a sample I should sit down and show him what I could do. My work was very good and when Bernstein saw what I could do he said all right you could start to work for yourself. That was when I took up my sister Minnie to work with me. She was only about four months in the country. … I had a third sister who worked on the 9th floor. A few months before the fire I told her to go away and find another job." - Celia Saltz, operator on the 8th Floor

One of those working at the factory on Saturday, March 25, 1911, was Celia Walker, who worked on the 9th floor as an examiner, a sort of quality control supervisor. She also felt she was different than many of the other girls working there: "When I worked in the Triangle shop all the other girls looked on me like I was a real 'Yankee'. When we came to this country I was only 5 years old and by the time I went to work in the shop I spoke with a real American accent. In the Triangle Co. I am sure that the girls thought I was American born. I worked on the 9th floor as an examiner. My job was to look over the work to see that it was made correctly - if it wasn't correct I got it back to the [Sewing Machine] Operators for fixing. I worked at the last table on the floor. In front of me were the rows of machines running in the same direction as my table. I could see clear across the shop. Way down in the front were the windows. I don't know if it was Washington or Greene Streets. To my left on the other wall were the windows to the other street."

Although women made up the majority of the employees, there were a handful of young men also working there, especially the more mechanical jobs. Though very young, Abe Gordon was taken on, and he talked about his experience there: "I was under 16 years old when I was recommended for the job as button-hole maker at the Triangle shop. I must have worked there three years before the fire. I worked on the 9th floor where there were about 400 machines. Bernstein, that dog, told me if I was good I could stay on. Well, I must have been good because after a few weeks they let me stay and I was getting $6 a week. I was a good worker -- I had my foot down on the button-hole machine even before the power was turned on. After a while someone told me to ask Bernstein in a nice way for a raise. I went to him and he said all right, I will give you 50¢ but don't tell anybody. I went back to the machine and they kept asking me, 'Did you get it, did you get it'. I answered back, 'Leave me alone'. I did not want to spoil it.

Ambitious, and with more opportunities available to him than those offered to the young women at that time, Gordon began working his way up through the business until he finally became a machinist: "I was mechanically inclined and I didn't like sitting at a machine too much -- I wanted to become a mechanic but first I had to become a belt boy. They asked me why I wanted to become a belt boy when I was making $6 and as the other I would make only $5. I went and saved up $12 and bought the head machinist an expensive watch fob. Then I became a belt boy. We always used the freight side of the shop. On the other side, door was always locked but there was a key on a string hanging from the lock. The machines were so close together that I had to go sideways to walk down the aisle. Bernstein was mean. I saw him pick up an operator by the shoulders and throw him out into the hall. Everybody kept their heads bent down over their machines."

In fact, by the time the fire started on March 25, 1911, many of those working at the Triangle Factory were catching a whiff of the change that was moving through manufacturing, especially in the large cities of the North. Worker were beginning to organize labor unions and use the clout that came from large numbers to get better pay and working conditions. Sylvia Kimeldorf, a tucker on the 8th floor, had been involved in the movement even before she came to work at the factory. She noted, "At that time I lived with my parents in Brooklyn. We had come from Rumania in 1901. I was 18 years old and had gone to work in the garment industry two years earlier and suddenly found that I was in the middle of the big 1909 strike of shirtwaist makers. I remember how I went to sell newspapers to raise money for the strikers. My cousin, Morris Horowitz took me up to work at Triangle."

Chapter 3: "It Was a Day Bursting with Life"

"It was a day that was bursting with life--a day full of the first breaths of spring and fate ruled that on this day, 146 young lives should be snuffed out in a terrible manner; they were destroyed by the horrible Triangle fire. ... The clock struck 8 o'clock, and we went to our machines. A cheerful feeling prevailed all over the floor. Perhaps it was because one of the girls came to work that day with a diamond ring which her fiancé had given her the night before. I remember that the girl's name was Esther; she was a very pretty and lively young lady, and on this occasion especially her joy was contagious, enveloping all around her. We who worked nearby were, as a result, feeling very content; we worked, sewed, joked, and were oblivious to the passage of time, unaware that it already was close to 12 o'clock." - Mary Domsky-Abrams, blouse operator on the 9th floor

March 25, 1911 was a Saturday, the last day of the work week, and it was nearly the end of the day by the time the fire started around 4:40 p.m. As a result, many of the workers had shut down their machines and gathered their belongings to leave, including Mary Domsky-Abrams. As she made clear, the timing of the fire allowed her to be one of the lucky survivors: "We were among the first ones to leave the ninth floor to go home. When we got to the back elevator (we would leave only by the back, only exit on one side, because the firm wanted to check on all workers to make sure they weren't taking anything out with them) we heard screams. At the elevator were two girls, orphans, who lived with their grandmother. One of them asked me, 'Mary, what's all the screaming about?' I told her it was like every time, everyone was shoving to get out first at the end of the day. … We still didn't know there was a fire. We were standing at the elevator, waiting for our friend Neda; she always wanted to leave by the elevator, while we usually didn't want to wait for the elevator and used to leave by the stairs. Neda arrived, and said: 'Mary, come quickly!' We took to the stairs, and when we got to the seventh floor, we saw the flames. The fire surged through the windows; everyone panicked, ran, screamed, and didn't know what to do. I became very frightened, and noticed that my friend was no longer with me. In the confusion, I attempted to run back upstairs, but someone stopped me. I don't remember how I got downstairs; I only had the feeling that a strong hand guided me. When I was in the street, I saw how people were jumping from the windows and falling like flies."

Although the Triangle Shirtwaist Factory fire is one of the most notorious events in New York City's history, it's still unclear exactly how the fire actually started. In the aftermath of the fire, there was speculation that the fire was started in a scrap bin by a lit cigarette butt, but Josephine Nicolosi, who made blouses on the 8th floor, may have been the first one to see the fire, and she later reported, "I was sitting and working. The pay envelopes were given out. The bell was ringing to go home and I was getting up. I worked near the cutting table facing the tables. A little match was burning on the table and Sal Marchesi, a cutter, he hollered to me 'Is a fire' - he used to joke all the time so I said, 'You are always fooling, it is only a little bit of a match.' But he took a pail, one of the red pails of water and threw it on the match. All of a sudden, as he threw the water, the flames shot up like an explosion. Right away the place was filled with fire and smoke and everybody was running around. I ran to the window and I was about to jump but I had not enough courage."

Nicolosi's comment is one of the most troubling of the testimonies about the fire because it implied that there was something in the bucket that caused the lit match to explode. This issue was later obscured in the hearings surrounding the incident since it was not considered the direct cause of death; the focus was fixated on the fact that certain factory doors were locked and thus prevented people from escaping in one of the building's two stairways. However, if Nicolosi's recollection was correct, it would seem that there was some sort of alcohol or other flammable liquid in the bucket that acted as an accelerant. Had some worker brought alcohol into the building and placed it in the water bucket so that they could surreptitiously drink on the job? Was this actually a wider spread practice that Sal Marchesi was unaware of when he threw the liquid on the match?

There is still no concrete answer for questions surrounding the origin of the fire, but there was no doubt that it spread fast and furiously. Sylvia Kimeldorf, who made the dainty tucks in the blouses that the factory produced, explained, "I remember the day of the fire very well. I was a tucker and I worked on the 8th floor where they had a number of special machines set up and I had just finished my work earlier in the day and I got my pay. I was always in a hurry as a youngster so I ran to the dressing room. I can remember as if it were yesterday that I had just put on my skirt and blouse and that I had my hat on, and that I put my jacket and pocketbook under my arm. At that moment I heard a commotion in back of me in the shop. I heard loud screaming coming from the other end of the shop. I turned around and I could see the flames at the other end of the shop. I had a very dear girl-friend by the name of Feibush and we worked together. She ran into the dressing room and grabbed me and began to pull me to the windows all the time while the fire was spreading quickly through the shop."

Celia Walker was working on the 9th floor and was not aware of any danger until the fire was quickly spreading. As it turned out, while the 8th floor could communicate with the 10th floor by telephone, there were no such accommodations for the 9th floor, and Walker explained how the crowded conditions on the 9th floor exacerbated the problem: "On the day of the fire I had gotten my clothes. I stood at my table ready to leave. I looked across the shop. In front of me I saw flames on the outside of the windows shooting up. The flames were climbing up from the 8th floor. I was scared and it seemed to me that even before I could move, everybody in the shop started to scream and holler. The girls at the machines began to climb up on the machine tables maybe because it was that they were frightened or maybe they thought they could run to the elevator doors on top of the machines. The aisles were narrow and blocked by the chairs and baskets. They began to fall in the fire. I know now that there was a fire escape in back of me but I ran to the elevator because that was the only place to run to."

Rose Hauser also worked on the 9th floor and witnessed the most egregious aspect of the fire: the infamous locked doors. "When I got out of the dressing room I looked toward the freight elevator and I saw smoke pouring up. The smoke was also coming out of the staircase. I ran with some of the other girls to the front door. I put my hand on the knob and tried to open it and I stood there screaming that the door was locked. I tried to open it and I stood there screaming that the door was locked. I tried to force it open with all my strength but it would not move. I looked around and I saw the flames coming in all the windows. The fire was in the shop and was coming toward us. There was a fire escape at the windows near the freight side. The fire escapes had iron doors and shutters. Everybody was running and hollering and people were choking from the heavy smoke. I took my muff and put it over my head. I ran back to the front elevator and there was no chance there. I kept my muff on my head and ran toward the freight side again. I found that the door to the back staircase was open and that is how I got out."

One of the workers, Kate Alterman, later testified about how a locked door led to the death of Margaret Schwartz: "I wanted to go up Greene street side, but the whole door was in flames, so I went in hid myself in the toilet rooms and bent my face over the sink, and then ran to the Washington side elevator, but there was a big crowd and I couldn't pass through there. I noticed someone, a whole crowd around the door, and I saw the Bernstein, the manager's brother trying to open the door, and there was Margaret near him. Bernstein tried the door, he couldn't open it and then Margaret began to open the door. I take her on one side I pushed her on the side and I said, 'Wait, I will open that door.' I tried, pulled the handle in and out, all ways--and I couldn't open it. She pushed me on the other side, got hold of the handle and then she tried. And then I saw her bending down on her knees, and her hair was loose, and the trail of her dress was a little far from her, and then a big smoke came and I couldn't see. I just know it was Margaret, and I said, 'Margaret,' and she didn't reply. I left Margaret, I turned my head on the side, and I noticed the trail of her dress and the ends of her hair begin to burn."

At first, it seemed that the fire might be stopped before it got too far. According to Sylvia Kimeldorf, "The fire started on the cutting table on the Washington Place side. ... I could see when I looked back at that time from the dressing room to where the lace runners worked, how the wicker baskets filled with the work, were already burning. I saw men throwing stuff on the fire trying to put it out."

However, the workers' attempts failed, and as the fire spread quickly, it induced panic as those inside tried to escape. Rose Indursky remembered, "When the fire began to rush on our floor we wanted to jump out of the window at first but somehow I kept my head while the others were fighting in the dark from the smoke. I kept saying to myself what all the greenhorns used to say, that in America they don't allow one to burn. I ran to the freight elevator side. The door there was open. When I got there the fire was all around me. The elevator had come up and the elevator man said there is a fire but he then went to the 10th floor for the bosses. ... When I went out into the hall staircase I bent down and looked downstairs and I could see the fire come up. In the shop the girls were running around with their hair burning…First I ran into the dressing room with the machinist and some of the others. Then the walls in the dressing room began to smoke. The machinist had a wild look in his eye. We ran back into the shop; girls were lying on the floor, fainted, and people were stepping on them. Some of the other girls were trying to climb over the machines. I remember the machinist ran to the window and he smashed it to let the smoke that was choking us go out. Instead, the flames rushed in. I stood at the window; across the street people were hollering "don't jump, don't jump." I turned around and ran to the hall staircase door. My hair was smoldering -- my clothes were torn. I put my two hands on my smoldering hair and ran up the stairs. I went into the 10th floor. Nobody was there except one man, bookkeeper. He was picking up papers and he hollered to me, can you come to the roof, can you come to the roof. By that time, all the windows on the 10th floor were burning. My life was saved on account of the bookkeeper. I didn't know that the next floor was the roof. I think if not for him I would have stayed on the 10th floor and maybe had been killed."

Dora Skalka, who worked on the 8th floor making blouses, was one of the fortunate ones who was near a door that opened. She explained, "I turned around and saw that the fire was already burning at the cutting table. My machine was in the first row next to the cutting table and if my girl-friend did not go home earlier, I am sure I would have been one of the first victims. But I was standing at the door of the dressing room with two or three other girls and we ran to the door of the Greene St. staircase. It was closed. All around me there was hollering. In a split second the place filled up with black smoke. I remained at the door. I did not move. I could not holler. I thought to myself at least I want to die by the door. I don't remember exactly how it happened but somebody opened the door from the outside. It was either a fireman or policeman who smashed in the door which was always locked. He grabbed us and told us to go down the staircase and he took us down to the 6th floor and left us there. He must have gone back upstairs. … I lost my coat and scarf in the fire. I remember that I began to go to the fire escape when I heard screaming. I knew there was a fire escape but then people began to holler that the fire escape had broken down. I wanted to run back into the shop but it got dark from the smoke in a split second."

A picture of horse-drawn firefighters heading for the burning factory

Chapter 4: "The Front Elevator Door"

"We could not open the front elevator door. Boxes next to the door made a narrow passage. Barrels near the freight stairway hall were filled with oil. They caught fire and must have blocked the way for others to escape. I didn't know there was a fire escape. We crossed from the roof into a window or door across the alley way. They put boards across. At the trial, all I could say was I did not know. I was scared and did not understand. … On the roof, I tried to hold back one girl who finally tore away from us and ran back downstairs to look for her sister. There was one girl on the roof who had saved herself by wrapping white goods all around her. She still had some of the goods around her." - Rose Indursky

Today, placards in every multi-storied building warn people not to take an elevator during a fire, but in 1911, elevators were still new and such warnings had not yet been put into place. Thus, it was only natural that most of those trying to escape ran toward the one elevator that they were allowed to use to exit the building each evening. In fact, they had no choice because the fire had spread to the main staircase, the other elevator couldn't be used, and the doors to the other staircase were locked. Sarah Friedman, who worked on the 9th floor, described the resulting scene: "There was a narrow vestibule leading to the freight elevator. I was waiting in that vestibule when all of a sudden the smoke, and then the fire, began to come up the elevator shaft. I turned to run back to the other end of the shop where the freight elevator was. I took one look into the shop as I ran and I saw the flames coming in from all sides. The elevators were going up and down. On the front side the door to the staircase was closed. I had to fight and push my way across the shop. There was screaming and shoving and many girls tried to climb over the machine tables."

Ethel Monick was one of the workers who managed to ride the elevator down while it still worked: "I ran to the freight elevator on the Greene St. side first but people were hollering that the cable broke. When I first came to work I was a lace cutter on the 9th floor. One day I was working and got lost in the shop near the Washington Place side. That was when I saw that there was a door there. In the fire, when I saw the freight elevator was down, then I thought of the Washington Place door. I ran to that door and tried to open it. All around me people were hollering, 'I am dying, I am dying.' I ran from the door into the dressing room looking for something to use on the door. In the dressing room there were men and women laughing. I did not know at the time that they were hysterical. I hollered, 'Let's get a machine head and smash the door in.' I remembered the top of the door was with wire glass. The door was absolutely locked. I went to the window on the Washington Place side. I wanted to fall out. Then I got ashamed about the way I would look. They pushed me back to the elevator and they pushed me right in."

It quickly became clear that the elevator was not going to move fast enough to take everyone down, which led some to make a fateful and desperate decision. Friedman continued, "The elevator had made several trips. I knew this was the last one but it was so loaded that the car started to go down. The door was not closed. Suddenly I was holding to the sides of the door looking down the elevator shaft with girls screaming and pushing behind me. It was the old style elevator -- cable elevator -- to make it go down, you pulled the cable from the floor up. That cable was at the side of the elevator shaft. I reached out and grabbed it. I remember sliding all the way down. I was the first one to slide down the shaft. I ended up on top of the elevator and then I lost consciousness. Others must have landed on top of me. When the rescue workers came to the shaft they pulled me out and laid me out on the street. I had a broken leg, broken arm. My skull had been injured. One of my hands had been burned by friction."

Celia Walker had a similar experience: "The door to the stairway was completely blocked by the big crates of blouses and goods. The fire crept closer to us and we were crowded at the elevator door banging and hollering for the elevator. The first time it came up, the girls rushed in and it was crowded in a half a second. The elevator driver struggled with the door and finally closed it and went down with the screaming girls. I was left with those who didn't make the first trip. Then the elevator came up a second time. The girls were all squeezing against the door and the minute it was opened they rushed again. This time I was sure I would be lucky and get in. I rushed with the other girls but just as I came to the door of the elevator it dropped down right in front of me. I could hear it rush down and I was left standing on the edge trying to hold myself back from falling into the shaft. I held on to the two sides of the open door. Behind me the girls were screaming and I could feel them pushing me more and more. I knew that in a few seconds I would be pushed into the shaft and I made a quick decision. Maybe through panic or maybe through instinct I saw the center cable of the elevator in front of me. I jumped and grabbed the cable. That is all I remember."

Eventually, the overcrowding on the elevator added to the tragedy. After making a few trips up and down, the stress of the added weight ultimately broke the elevator's cable, sending the last load of passengers plummeting to the ground.

Pictures of some of the damage

Chapter 5: "Word Had Spread…by Some Magic Terror"

"One Saturday afternoon in March of that year — March 25, to be precise — I was sitting at one of the reading tables in the old Astor Library… I was deeply engrossed in my book when I became aware of fire engines racing past the building. By this time I was sufficiently Americanized to be fascinated by the sound of fire engines. Along with several others in the library, I ran out to see what was happening, and followed crowds of people to the scene of the fire. A few blocks away, the Asch Building at the corner of Washington Place and Greene Street was ablaze. When we arrived at the scene, the police had thrown up a cordon around the area and the firemen were helplessly fighting the blaze. The eighth, ninth, and tenth stories of the building were now an enormous roaring cornice of flames. Word had spread through the East Side, by some magic of terror, that the plant of the Triangle Waist Company was on fire and that several hundred workers were trapped." - Louis Waldman, a politician who later became a New York State Assemblyman

The workers who didn't have access to the roof or any means of escape seemingly had to choose between jumping out the window or staying inside and burning alive or being overcome by smoke, but Ida Kornweiser, an operator and sleeve setter from the ninth floor, took a terrible chance in order to escape the flames and was incredibly lucky that it paid off: "I had my pay money in my hand. I don't know what made me do it but right there I bent over and pushed my pay into the top of my stocking. Then I ran into the staircase hall but the flames were coming up from downstairs. I tried to get through but I could not. There was too much heat. I ran back into the shop. I don't know where it came from but I found a roll of lawn piece goods maybe it wasn't a whole roll. It was white lawn. I wrapped it around and around and around me until only my face showed out. Then I ran right into the fire in the stair way hall. I ran upstairs. I gasped for breath. The lawn caught fire as I ran and I kept peeling it off of me. I kept turning and twisting while I was running because the burning lawn was on me."

Eventually some people were able to break a door or two open and make their way down the crowded staircase, but even those who reached the streets safely were soon surrounded by new horrors. Rose Hauser was one of the ones fortunate enough to live to tell the tale: "Before I went down the staircase I looked to the fire escape. I saw one woman climb on there and fall right over the rail. When I began to go down to the 8th floor, I was choking. The fire was in the hall on the 8th floor. I put my muff around my head tightly and I ran right through the fire. The fur caught on fire. When we got down stairs they kept us in the hall and they wouldn't let us go into the street because the bodies were falling down. The firemen finally came and took us out across the street and we stood numb in the doorway of a Chinese import store. I saw one woman jump and get caught on a hook on the 6th floor and watched how a fireman saved her. The elevators were the old fashioned cable car kind with the cable going right through the car. I wasn't hysterical and I was just numb. After all this horror I remember I finally met my girl-friend. She did not know about the fire and she scolded me for being late. We never went to buy the hat."

Similarly, when Sylvia Kimeldorf made it to the first floor of the building, she was told not to leave because there was as much danger outside as there was indoors: "I don't remember how I got down that narrow staircase but I was cold, wet and hysterical. I was screaming all the time. When we came to the bottom I could not get out of the building. The firemen held us back in the doorway. The bodies were falling all around us and they were afraid to let us go out because we would be killed by the falling bodies. I stood there with the other girls screaming until the men saw a chance for us to get across and I remember they let me across the street and took me into a Chinese importing house where they tried to quiet me down and gave me milk to drink. I could see through the window how the bodies were still falling and would hit the sidewalk with a bounce. … When I was able to get out of the store I began to run all the way to Second Street and Avenue 'A' where my grandmother lived. My mother in Brooklyn had no telephone and I was afraid she would think something happened to me. My grandma took care of me. Meanwhile my cousin was frantically looking for me even among the dead bodies."

As is usually the case with an accident or disaster, bystanders began to gather outside the building, drawn there by the noise and the sense of excitement. Eraclio Montanaro worked down the street from the Triangle Factory and mentioned what he saw: "My friend and I worked in a tailor shop on 4th Avenue, and 11th St. That day when we stopped after a half day's work, it was such a nice day, like in April, that we decided to take a walk to Broadway and Canal. When we came to Wanamakers we turned into Waverly Place. We heard an uproar and we saw people running so we ran too. Then we saw what was happening at the corner of Washington and Greene Streets. For a while we couldn't move. We watched in horror how bunches of women came hurtling down from the top stories of the building. The firemen were helpless. The nets were ripped from the hands. Many stooped and picked up the nets again with their hands bleeding. My friend collapsed and started to cry like a woman. All around us we saw people covered with blood. I got sick and could not look any more."

Even those who had never set foot in the Triangle were shocked by what they were seeing. Louis Waldman later told one man, "Horrified and helpless, the crowds…looked up at the burning building, saw girl after girl appear at the reddened windows, pause for a terrified moment, and then leap to the pavement below, to land as mangled, bloody pulp. This went on for what seemed a ghastly eternity. Occasionally a girl who had hesitated too long was licked by pursuing flames and, screaming with clothing and hair ablaze, plunged like a living torch to the street. Life nets held by the firemen were torn by the impact of the falling bodies. The emotions of the crowd were indescribable. Women were hysterical, scores fainted; men wept as, in paroxysms of frenzy, they hurled themselves against the police lines."

Waldman

Chapter 6: "The Screams and Sobs All Around Were Deafening"

A newspaper picture of victims on the ground

"The tragedy was even greater because of the fact that the fireman's ladders were too short and couldn't reach the ninth and tenth floors. Also, the nets spread to catch the jumpers were too weak, and many plunged right through to their deaths. I saw a number of firemen crying as they witnessed victims of the fire killed as they broke through the nets. A forelady from the ninth floor, whom I knew well and who that day had told me she was preparing work for me for Monday, jumped from the high floor and was saved by her coat catching on a hook at the sixth floor, and she remained hanging there. In the confusion, I watched the fire and saw how the rescue operation was conducted under conditions of panic. Flames poured through the windows of the top floors and thick smoke billowed. ...I saw that, besides ambulances, they were bringing caskets. The screams and sobs all around were deafening. Water was being poured onto the flames, the firemen and police were doing their utmost, but they were not prepared for so overwhelming an emergency, and consequently the number of victims was so large." - Mary Domsky-Abrams

Frank Rubino was among the first firefighters at the scene of the conflagration and reported how the fire department's response began: "The alarm came in at 4:45 P.M. from Fire Box #289 which is at the corner of Greene and Washington. ... The first alarm came in by a phone call from people in the building across the street. ... As we turned the corner the first thing I saw was a body of a man come falling down, landing on the roof of the shed and crashing right through. We kept going and turned into Greene St. and began to stretch out to the hook up to the stand pipe. I was working with John P. Crawford and he was trying to make the connection. Then I saw the bodies begin to come down on the sidewalk and I hollered to him, 'Come out of there, come out of there, you will get killed.' Those bodies were coming down with the force of 1 1/2 tons by the time they hit the sidewalk. They were coming down with hair and clothes burning - you know the girls at that time wore long hair. When the bodies didn't crash through the deadlights, they lay there on the sidewalk three or four high, burning, and we had to play the hoses on them." Shockingly, even the falling bodies spread the fire, as Rubino pointed out: "While we were upstairs, we had others who were fighting another fire in the cellar. Some of the falling bodies crashed through the dead lights and went into the cellar which was stored with rabbits' fur and set that on fire. We had to lay out lines in the cellar."

Ironically, the building housing the factory was relatively new at less than a decade old, and it actually had some excellent firefighting equipment built into its infrastructure. Rubino noted that "standpipes (a sort of indoor fire hydrant) were not required by law at this time but this building had them and it reduced insurance on the building." Unfortunately, the fire spread so fast that even these features were not terribly helpful. He continued, "We finally made the connection and went up the stairway, 8 floors. Some of the other men had gotten up as high as the 10th and they tried using the standpipes on the 10th floor. There was a crossover there of the pipes and the whole thing had crashed down. By the time we were coming up the steps there was a steady flow of water coming down."

As is so often the case, it was left to the firefighters to make some of the most shocking discoveries of the fire. Rubino recalled, "We had to break the door in to get in. There was a partition on the inside around the door. Behind the partition, the bodies were piled up. When we hit them with the hose, they just broke down and crumbled. There were 25 to 30 bodies piled up at the back windows."

Pictures of firefighters standing among victims

Like the firefighters, everyone wanted to help but soon realized there was little they could do. Rubino explained, "The civilians helped us with nets but it was no good because as many as 5 or 6 bodies came down at one time. We had tall ladders at the scene. Hook and Ladder Company number 20 from Mercer Street came in with a 90 feet, ladder but that was straight up. When you backed away from the building, of course, it got shorter. One of the men crept along the ledge to the corner of the building and perched himself behind the Triangle Shirtwaist sign like it was a shield. There was nothing we could do once they began to jump. People began to holler, 'Raise the ladders, raise the ladders.' But we had the ladders up - they don't know that it is more important in such a situation to hose back the fire so you can save lives. But once they began to jump there is nothing we could do. … They came out the windows because they were being pushed by those in back of them who were being burned by the fire. That was not panic - there was nothing else they could do but go out the window."

One of the most amazing stories of rescue was told by Frank H. Sommer, a professor at the New York University Law School housed next door. He later told a reporter, "I remember it was about 5 o'clock. I was lecturing to a class of about fifty boys. All was quiet and serene, when suddenly we heard the toot of whistles and the sound of gongs and fire engines. I threw open the door of the lecture room, and then the door of the Law School Faculty room, which opens on an areaway separating our building from the burning one. Some of the boys followed me, and we saw the ten-story building across the areaway was on fire. The open space between us and that building was filled with smoke. There were ear-piercing shrieks, and girls appeared at the windows of the lofts in which was the waist factory. We hurried to the roof of our building, where two ladders had been left by painters, and the boys used these in the work of rescue. They worked like beavers, apparently never giving a thought to the possibility that their own building might catch fire from the flames that were leaping out into the open space. How it was done I don't know, but in surprisingly short time about fifty girls were brought across the ladders to safety. The boys paid no attention to the thick smoke and risked life and limb to steady the terror-stricken girls on the ladders. Some of the rescued were pitiable sights. In some cases it was necessary to beat out the flames that had caught their clothing, and many of them had blackened faces and singed hair and eyebrows. But our heroes were not ready to desert even after they had all of the girls in places of safety. They manned the standpipe and hose in our building and did efficient work, and other ran out to get the firemen to come in and save our property. As it was, the flames swept across the areaway, cracked the plate glass in our windows, and set fire to several of the rooms. Many books, papers, and documents were lugged out of the building by the volunteer workers."

The law students were not the only heroic civilians who sprang into action either. Mary Domsky-Abrams also mentioned that one group of men "made a human ladder of themselves in an attempt to make it possible for girls hunched in fear at the windows not yet on fire to cross over to the next building, to which there was a small bridge (or passage.) But all the men, about 10 of them, fell down, not being able to bear up under the weight, and were killed together with those who tried to save themselves. We were all deeply moved by the heroism and tried to kiss their bodies as they were being removed to the morgue."

The scene outside the building after the fire

A picture of bodies being placed in temporary coffins

Chapter 7: "The Rules of the Institutions Were Suspended"

"To these hospitals, as well as to Bellevue, where there were two survivors last night, crowds of relatives and friends of the injured and others who had been searching for hours without success for someone known to be in the building when the fire occurred and not accounted for, steadily streamed yesterday. If the physicians decided that the injured were strong enough to be seen the rules of the institutions were suspended for these visitors. Most of those in the hospitals received their injuries by jumping from the windows." - *New York Times*, March 27, 1911

Many of those who survived the fire were shocked they weren't dead when they woke up in a hospital, a sentiment expressed by Celia Walker: "My next thing I knew was when I opened my eyes and I was lying on my back and I looked up into the faces of a priest and a nun who were trying to help me. I was in St. Vincent's Hospital. Everybody thought I was going to die. They found me at the bottom of the shaft. I had saved myself by my jumping. Others had fallen down the shaft on top of me and I suppose I was found by the firemen when they were removing the dead. I have often wondered how I was saved. I was very lucky. By sliding down the cable I was far enough away from where most of the bodies landed on top of the elevator cage as they fell down the shaft. My head was injured and I had a broken arm and a broken finger. I had a large searing scar down the middle of my body, burned by the friction of the cable which had cut through my clothing. In the hospital, later, I was shown a large ripped piece of fur and fabric."

To her credit, Walker was modest about her heroic survival, later admitting, "One of the nurses said she thought it was wonderful that I had enough presence of mind when I jumped to wrap something around my hands in order to save them and to be able to hold on to the cable. I know it was not presence of mind or courage. I think the right word is vanity. This was a new muff that I had bought after saving for it many weeks and fire or no fire, something in me made me hold on to it even while I jumped to save my life. I don't know how long I stayed in St. Vincent's but when I was well the Red Cross came with my clothing which they got from my family and took me straight to the mountains for a rest. At the same time, the Red Cross paid my family $10 a week for 10 weeks. I never got a dime's worth of help from the company."

As soon as they were out of the building, most of the survivors ran immediately to their homes. This may strike some as odd today, but most of these young workers were only first generation or second generation Americans who had grown up in tight-knit communities. With no access to telephones or other methods of contacting relatives, they were anxious that their families not hear about the fire and become unnecessarily upset by having to fear the worst. For instance, Rose Hauser said, "My cousin was going home from work when he heard about the fire. He rushed to my house. He lived on Lewis St. He cried out that he did not know what to do, that he did not see me and he asked my mother where was Rose. I was in the other room in what must have been a state of shock. My mother asked him (Harry) what was the matter and he began to tell her about the fire. I came out of the room and stood there listening to him and I could feel my mother become more and more excited. When he told her what happened she fainted and collapsed to the floor. It was only then that I also began to cry and I cried for hours. The next day there was a regular parade of people. They all came to see me and I was still alive. The full tragedy hit me at that time. I could not sleep for weeks."

Tragically, not everyone was as fortunate as Hauser's mother: "We had a 'landlady' -- I was very friendly with her daughter who was their only child and who worked in Triangle. When the 'landlady' heard that I had been saved she came yelling into our house and in her sorrow began to wave her hands at me and berate me why I had not saved her daughter. The poor woman -- she lost her mind. My mother pleaded with her and tried to calm her. For a long time after that I was afraid to walk on the block where she lived. I was afraid to meet her. I dreamed about it at night and I would dream that I was falling out of the window screaming -- the whole house would wake up. I remember hollering to my mother in the dark, 'Mama, I just jumped out of the window.'"

Hauser was hardly the only one traumatized by the fire. Ethel Monick admitted that she couldn't believe the fire was reality, even as she was living it: "When I got to the street I kept murmuring to myself, 'It's all a bad dream,' and I started to scratch my face and tear my hair because something in me said that would wake me up. I remember a newspaper man took me under my arm. He was from the Journal. He asked me, 'What is the matter,' and I said, 'There were 150 girls up there who will never get out.' He took me to a subway. It was the first time I was in a subway because I always went home by the Third Ave. El. My father would give me a nickel to go to work, a nickel to come home and a nickel for lunch. The night of the fire I got home late. I got a licking from my father. He called me a 'bummike' and my mother stood in the corner shivering. I kept hollering, 'But Pa.' but he would not listen and I had to go to sleep. I guess while I was sleeping, they found out the truth because when I got up they were all standing around me and kissing me."

Chapter 8: "We Mourned Our Dead Comrades"

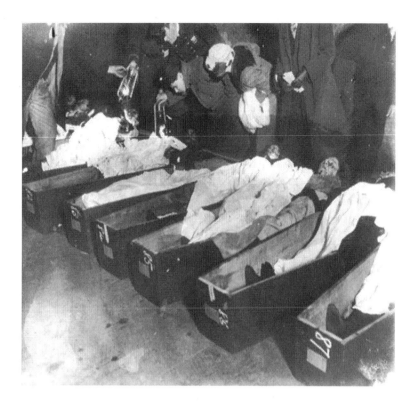

Pictures of people trying to identify victims at the morgue

"That spring of 1911 we mourned our dead comrades, the victims of a society which was concerned only with the profits of an individual and not with the welfare of the many, of the working masses. The Triangle victims were martyrs in the fight for social justice, and the labor movement will always remember them as those who, with their young lives, paved the way for a better world with a more just society, a world free from exploitation, in which equal rights for all will be respected." - Mary Domsky-Abrams

It has since been established that 146 people died by burning, suffocating, jumping, or a combination of the three, but in the wake of the disaster, it was unclear how many victims there were. One lengthy New York Times headline read, "DEATH LIST IS 141; ONLY 86 IDENTIFIED But Several More of the Injured in the Hospital are Expected to Succumb. 22 BEYOND RECOGNITION Thirteen of the Dead Were Men -- All the Rest Women -- the Coroner's Summary." The article then went on to report, "When all the bodies of the victims of Saturday's fire had been counted, recounted, and checked by officials of the Coroner's office Coroner Holtzhauser made official announcement last night that the total number of the dead was 141. Of this number 133 were found at the scene of the fire, either out on the sidewalk or huddled on the ninth floor of the factory building. Three died of their injuries in Bellevue

Hospital, there in St. Vincent's Hospital, and two in New York Hospital. The total number identified at midnight was seventy-eight at the Morgue; eight dead in hospitals. The unidentified still number 33. Of these 28 are women and 5 men. The other bodies are hopelessly charred and probably never will be identified. The total number of women who lost their lives in the fire, according to the Coroner's figures, is 128; the number of men is 13."

The newspapers continued to release information about the catastrophe and tried to update people on the status of both the victims and the survivors. Under an article titled "FIVE DYING IN HOSPITALS; Seven Others Who Are Less Badly Injured Being Cared For," the *Times* reported, "At the hospitals to which the victims of the Triangle waist fire were taken, it was stated last night that at least five more will probably die. The total number of survivors at the hospitals last night was twelve. Three women who are in St. Vincent's Hospital are believed to be hopelessly injured. They are Sarah Kupla, 18…Esther Harris, 21…whose back is broken, and Annie Miller, 17…who has a fractured leg and internal injuries. Five others at this hospital are expected to recover. In the New York Hospital are Freda Valakowsky, 20 years old…with a fractured leg and internal injuries, and Mrs. Daisy Fitze…who has a compound fracture of the pelvic bone. Neither of these is likely to recover. … One of the most pathetic scenes was the identification by her brother Louis of the body of Becky Nerberer of 19 Clinton Street, at the New York hospital. Nerberer had inquired at the hospital Saturday night about his sister's condition and was told that she had a chance to live. He returned at 3 o'clock yesterday morning and found her dead. He was so crazed with grief that attendants had to hold him. He said that his parents were expected to arrive in this country from Russia within a few weeks, and that passage money had been sent to them from his savings."

Of course, the tragedy did not end with the fire; in fact, it dragged on for weeks as families attempted to identify and bury their dead. Among the most difficult situations were those faced by Jewish relatives whose faith required them to bury their loved ones within 24 hours of their deaths. This was often not possible because it took time and effort to identify the bodies.

When the funerals were held, they were attended by masses of people. Mary Domsky-Abrams remembered, "Later I went to visit the parents of Esther, who just before the tragedy had been given a ring by her fiancé. The father thanked God that his son, who also had worked at Triangle, had survived. The Mother was broken up, and she told us that Friday night her daughter was radiantly happy; she had played a Russian record on the phonograph, *I Didn't Come to Say Goodbye*, and the girl, had sung along so heartily... The funeral took place several days after the tragedy. All New York--certainly, all of Jewish New York--came to the funeral. The funeral procession was most moving. These young people--mainly young Jewish girls, pretty as pictures, were being brought to their eternal rest. Practically all of them were to be married soon, most of them had fiancés among the youthful community, their parents also were quite young, people in early middle age. Choked sobs were heard all around. The people were crying, the streets were crying--and the skies also were crying that day. Just as if heaven and earth were taking part in the tragedy, on that day of the funeral it was a pouring rain. You could touch the sorrow in the air."

Pictures of a procession held in honor of the victims

Moreover, for those who survived or witnessed the fire, the emotional scars lasted long after the physical wounds were gone. Rose Indursky later admitted, "For a long time after the fire I used to have nightmares and shake in my sleep when I dreamt of it. Many times during the day, if I would hear a fire engine I would begin to feel faint and I remember a long time after when we used to have fire drills, every time there was a fire drill I used to get sick."

To add insult to injury, the Triangle Company tried to get by without paying many of those injured what they were owed. Indursky explained, "You know the company held in one week's pay -- then we had to go get the pay. Many were afraid to come for the pay but it was only when we went to the University Place shop to get our pay that we began to see who was saved. While we were waiting we saw a father, mother, sister or brother and we asked who was dead and who was alive; so we knew. I was 16 years old at the time."

Chapter 9: Investigations and Reforms

"I would be a traitor to these poor burned bodies if I came here to talk good fellowship. We have tried you good people of the public and we have found you wanting.... We have tried you citizens; we are trying you now, and you have a couple of dollars for the sorrowing mothers, brothers and sisters by way of a charity gift. But every time the workers come out in the only way they know to protest against conditions which are unbearable, the strong hand of the law is allowed to press down heavily upon us. Public officials have only words of warning to us—

warning that we must be intensely peaceable, and they have the workhouse just back of all their warnings. The strong hand of the law beats us back, when we rise, into the conditions that make life unbearable. I can't talk fellowship to you who are gathered here. Too much blood has been spilled. I know from my experience it is up to the working people to save themselves. The only way they can save themselves is by a strong working-class movement." - Rose Schneiderman, a socialist, speaking at the memorial meeting held in the Metropolitan Opera House on April 2, 1911.

Schneiderman

A chance to pay their respects to the dead brought about healing and some sort of closure for many, but for others, it was only through political activism that they were able to make sense of the tragedy and ensure that the victims didn't die in vain. Martha Bensley Bruere, a union activist, recorded her thoughts in the wake of the tragedy: "Well, the fire is over, the girls are dead, and as I write, the procession in honor of the unidentified dead is moving by under my windows. … And still as I write the mourning procession moves past in the rain. For two hours they have been going steadily by and the end is not yet in sight. There have been no carriages, no imposing marshals on horseback; just thousands and thousands of working men and women carrying the banners of their trades through the long three-mile tramp in the rain. Never have I seen a military pageant or triumphant ovation so impressive; for it is not because 146 workers were killed in the Triangle shop - not altogether. It is because every year there are 50,000 working men and women killed in the United States - 136 a day; almost as many as happened to be killed together on the 25th of March; and because slowly, very slowly, it is dawning on these thousands on thousands that such things do not have to be! It is four hours later and the last of the procession has just passed."

Pictures of marches commemorating the victims

Meanwhile, following the publicity around the fire, and the outcry it caused, the State of New

York filed charges against Isaac Harris and Max Blanck, the owners of the Triangle Shirtwaist Company. The trial lasted for days, with more than 100 former employees of the company testifying about the circumstances surrounding the fire. Many testified consistently of the locked doors and the cries for help, while others apparently succumbed to bribery. Josephine Nicolosi, the blouse maker who had worked on the 8th floor, asserted, "Blank offered me $1,000 to change my testimony. You know the company held back one week's pay all the time. That is why after the fire we had to go to an empty store - I don't remember where - to collect the pay the company held back. He said to me, 'Come here you. Why you say the door's locked.' I said to him, 'That is the truth.' He said, 'How much do you want.' I screamed to the police, 'He wants me to cheat my friends.'"

Likewise, Abe Gordon later admitted, "I stayed with them (Harris & Blank) -- they went to Waverly Place. I knew they needed witnesses and I remember one day they called me into the office. There was a short thin man there. I was a 'greener' but he called me Mr. Gordon and he tried to put me at ease. This was the lawyer Max Steuer. He talked to me. He didn't tell me what to say but the way he talked to me I knew what he wanted. He said, for example, 'Mr. Gordon, isn't it true that most of the time you saw the key handing there'. 'Mr. Gordon, isn't it true you could use that door if you wanted to.' I was never a witness but we used to go down to the court to wait in case someone was called."

The trial itself was quite an ordeal for the witnesses, most of whom only knew English as a second language, and some of the workers who testified in the case discussed the tactics employed by the lawyer for the defendants and his attempts to impeach witnesses' testimony without explicitly attacking their credibility. Rose Hauser remembered, "I was one of the first witnesses called. Steuer (the attorney for the defense) certainly made me sweat. He put words in my mouth. He confused me and tried to prove I was lying. I said one word and he twisted it to mean its opposite. He prodded me and while I answered him I could see in front of me, the bodies of the girls falling through the air but he was trying to make me look like a fool. At one point I screamed out at him, 'I am not lying, I am telling the truth. For god sakes I could see the whole thing in front of me.' I could have killed him. I could have scratched his eyes out. I testified about the door being closed. I told them I tried the door in the front. There were about 150 girls on the floor. It was a long dressing room but when five girls were in it, it looked crowded. It had a sink, toilets but no cot."

Mary Domsky-Abrams was also upset by the defense's tactics: "I retorted, heatedly, that they should be ashamed of spreading such slanders. The fact was that, even if the workers had wanted to steal anything, it would have been impossible, because when bundles of work were distributed, every item was counted and listed on the tickets. And when the work was completed, everything was counted again. The bosses lawyers made all sorts of excuses, attempting to defend the employers on keeping the door locked, in face of another girl's testimony that even when the fire already had broken out, and she was among the first to reach the elevator, she had to show the watchman the contents of her pocketbook..."

In the end, Steuer's tactics worked, and it's believed the turning point came when Steuer had Kate Alterman, who testified about how a locked door led to the death of Margaret Schwartz, repeat her testimony several times. By pointing out that Alterman's accounts were almost identical as she continued to answer his questions, Steuer was able to insinuate that Alterman had been coached to memorize her testimony, thus casting doubt on its authenticity. As Mary Domsky-Abrams put it, "The Triangle Company bosses went free. 'Justice' found them not guilty. In those days--and also today--there was no proper measure of justice for lives of workers. The Triangle Company was found not guilty, though it had been responsible in the fire that snuffed out 147 lives. But this same 'justice' later condemned the martyrs Sacco and Vanzetti, because they hadn't killed anyone and had fought for true justice. But although the Triangle bosses were let off, apparently their consciences must have bothered them, or else they wished to temper the wrath that was aroused at them. They sent agents to the parents of the victims, or to other relatives, and offered them a certain sum of money as a reparation for their loss. I know there were some who accepted this money. The company claimed it was giving this money to help support the survivors or to give them an opportunity to go to the 'country' to recover from their experiences. They thought they could pay off their crimes in this way. When the company agents came to me with their money offer, Abrams, then my young comrade (now my deceased husband), showed them the door."

Perhaps the most perverse result of all was that the bosses actually made money off the fire. After the two owners were acquitted, a civil suit found them liable in the amount of $75 for each dead worker, but the insurance company covered damages that amounted to $400 per dead worker, meaning Harris and Blanck actually made about $60,000 in the process.

That said, while the victims never received true justice, the fire itself did create a blaze in the Worker's Union movement, and it burned steadily for the next several decades. In the wake of the disaster, the city's leaders began passing laws that limited the number of hours a worker could be required to work each week and raising the amount of money they were paid per hour. The government also passed one law after another increasing the minimum age for children workers and created many regulations improving factory safety, especially once the city's fire chief warned that hundreds of factories had conditions similar to the Triangle Shirtwaist Factory. In that sense, the 123 women and 23 men who died on March 25, 1911 became martyrs for a greater cause in which many of them dearly believed: the right of each American worker to have a safe and decent place in which to earn a living.

Bibliography

Auch, Mary Jane (2002). Ashes of Roses. Henry Holt Books for Young Readers. ISBN 0-8050-6686-1.

Haddix, Margaret Peterson (2007). Uprising. Simon & Schuster Children's Publishing. ISBN 978-1-4169-1171-5.

Kolen, Amy (Spring 2001). "Fire". The Massachusetts Review 42 (1): 13–36. JSTOR 25091716.

Sosinsky, Leigh (2011). The New York City Triangle Factory Fire. Charleston, South Carolina: Arcadia Publishing. ISBN 978-0-7385-7403-5

Stein, Leon (1962). *The Triangle Fire*. Cornell University Press.

von Drehle, David (2003). *Triangle: The Fire That Changed America*. New York: Atlantic Monthly Press.

Made in the USA
San Bernardino, CA
01 April 2018